That Little Something

Also by Charles Simic

That Little Something

Poems

Charles Simic

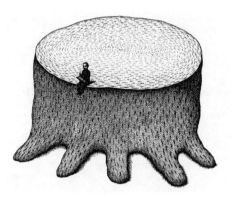

HARCOURT, INC.

Orlando ★ Austin ★ New York ★ San Diego ★ London

Excerpt from "Dance of the Macabre Mice" from *The Collected Poems
of Wallace Stevens* by Wallace Stevens. Reprinted by permission of Knopf.

Publication acknowledgments appear on page 75
and constitute a continuation of the copyright page.

Title page art by Peter Sís

Library of Congress Cataloging-in-Publication Data
Simic, Charles, 1938–
That little something: poems/Charles Simic.—1st ed.
p.   cm.
I. Title.
PS3569.I4725T47   2008
811'.54—dc22   2007032812
ISBN 978-0-15-101359-3

Text set in Dante
Designed by Cathy Riggs

Printed in the United States of America
First edition
A C E G I K J H F D B

CONTENTS

I

II

III

IV

That Little Something

I

WALKING

I never run into anyone from the old days.
It's summer and I'm alone in the city.
I enter stores, apartment houses, offices
And find nothing remotely familiar.

The trees in the park—were they always so big?
And the birds so hidden, so quiet?
Where is the bus that passed this way?
Where are the greengrocers and hairdressers,

And that schoolhouse with the red fence?
Miss Harding is probably still at her desk,
Sighing as she grades papers late into the night.
The bummer is, I can't find the street.

All I can do is make another tour of the neighborhood,
Hoping I'll meet someone to show me the way
And a place to sleep, since I've no return ticket
To wherever it is I came from earlier this evening.

THAT LITTLE SOMETHING

for Li-Young Lee

The likelihood of ever finding it is small.
It's like being accosted by a woman
And asked to help her look for a pearl
She lost right here in the street.

She could be making it all up,
Even her tears, you say to yourself,
As you search under your feet,
Thinking, Not in a million years . . .

It's one of those summer afternoons
When one needs a good excuse
To step out of a cool shade.
In the meantime, what ever became of her?

And why, years later, do you still,
Off and on, cast your eyes to the ground
As you hurry to some appointment
Where you are now certain to arrive late?

THE ELEVATOR IS OUT OF ORDER

Grandmothers and their caged birds
Must be trembling with fear
As you climb with heavy steps,
Stopping at each floor to take a rest.

A monkey dressed in baby clothes,
Who belonged to an opera singer,
Once lived here and so did a doctor
Who peddled drugs to wealthy customers.

The one who let you feel her breasts
Vanished upstairs. The name is not familiar,
But the scratches of her nails are.
The bell rings, but no one comes to open the door.

That old man, with a face powdered white,
You caught peeking out of a door,
Whom did he expect to see if not you,
All frazzled and descending in a hurry?

NIGHT CLERK IN A ROACH HOTEL

I'm the furtive inspector of dimly lit corridors,
Dead light bulbs and red exit signs,
Doors that show traces
Of numerous attempts at violent entry,

Is that the sound of a maid making a bed at midnight?
The rustle of counterfeit bills
Being counted in the wedding suite?
A fine-tooth comb passing through a head of gray hair?

Eternity is a mirror and a spider web,
Someone wrote with lipstick in the elevator.
I better get the passkey and see for myself.
I better bring along a book of matches too.

SOUVENIRS OF HELL

Empty beer cans tied to an old model car.
A small circus tent in a parking lot.
Sparrows chirping in rows of trees
That have never known leaves.

The stores on Main Street were boarded up,
Except for a brightly lit tattoo parlor.
Persephone's daughters on show
With orange hair and spiked collars.

You wish to know about the fires?
We saw mills the color of dried blood
Half-shadowed, half-lit by the setting sun,
Their many windows mostly broken.

The drunk who asked for spare change,
Wanted to tell us about his time in prison,
But with Satan's palace still to see,
We left him right there with his mouth open.

DRAMATIC EVENINGS

You take turns being yourself,
Being someone else,
Addressing mirrors, airing your grievances
To a goldfish in a bowl.
Your Queen Gertrude and Ophelia
Are snoring away across town.
Your father's ghost is in the bathroom
Reading *Secret Life of Nuns,*

While you pace back and forth
Clenching and unclenching your fists,
As if planning a murder,
Or more likely your own crucifixion.
Or you stand frozen still
As if an idea so obvious, so grand
Has come to you
And left you, for once, speechless.

Outside, you notice, it has started snowing.
You press your feverish forehead
Against the cold windowpane
And watch the flakes come down
Languidly, one at a time,
On the broken bird feeder and the old dog's grave.

DEPARTMENT OF COMPLAINTS

Where you are destined to turn up
Some dark winter day
Walking up and down dead escalators
Searching for someone to ask
In this dusty old store
Soon to close its doors forever.

At long last, finding the place, the desk
Stacked high with sales slips,
Concealing the face of the one
You came to complain to
About the coat on your back,
Its frayed collar, the holes in its pockets.

Recalling the stately fitting room,
The obsequious salesman, the grim tailor
Who stuck pins in your shoulders
And made chalk marks on your sleeves
As you admired yourself in a mirror,
Your fists clenched fiercely at your side.

TO BOREDOM

I'm the child of your rainy Sundays.
I watched time crawl
Over the ceiling
Like a wounded fly.

A day would last forever,
Making pellets of bread,
Waiting for a branch
On a bare tree to move.

The silence would deepen,
The sky would darken,
As Grandmother knitted
With a ball of black yarn.

Heaven is like that.
In eternity's classrooms,
The angels sit like bored children
With their heads bowed.

DEATH'S BOOK OF JOKES

Eager to explain how the wristwatch works
As he shadows me on the street.
He could be the Grim Reaper because he wears black,
Is pale-faced and grimly officious.

The clock on the old Unitarian church
Had stopped at five to eleven.
The one over the Savings Bank
Said it was exactly three o'clock

When he came after me with his watch,
Whose gothic numerals and absence of hands
He wanted me to inspect and admire
Before I burst out laughing at its price.

FIORDILIGI

My mother sang opera all day long.
She made beds, scrambled eggs,
And swore that not even death
Could change her heart's devotion.

Her voice like an air-raid siren.
Her voice—the soft evening rain.
In the shed, the rabbits trembled,
The rooster looked up admiringly at her.

Days of ecstasy, anguish, silence.
Days of long black dresses,
Of dozen white handkerchiefs
Crumpled and strewn all over the house.

One time we took a walk in the cemetery.
The leafless old trees terrified me
And so did her hands clenched into fists
As her arms rose higher and higher.

Grocers and mailmen ran from her
As from a sleepwalker
Who came after them in broad daylight
Pleading for news of her lost love.

DEVIL AND EVE

We were school chums.
Coatless, frozen stiff
We diddled the hours away,
Licking snowflakes
As they slid down our faces.

The bare-legged one
Who tagged along
Blowing on her fingers
Called herself Eve—
Wouldn't you know it!

We sat in a stolen car
With me hunched at the wheel
Peering through the windshield
At a police cruiser,
While the lovebirds

Went on doing whatever
It was they were doing in the backseat,
Trying not to titter
As they swore
Each other to secrecy.

THE LATE GAME

That sleepwalking waiter
Carrying plates of burgers and fries,
Is he coming to our table,
Or is he going to walk out of this place?
He's going to walk right out.

A baseball game played under the lights
In a small field across the road
Has gone past midnight
Because the score is tied,
And now someone's hungry

In the near-empty bleachers,
Or out in the back
Where couples make out in the bushes
Young boys smoke reefers,
And take long pees side by side.

WAITING FOR THE SUN TO SET

These rows of tall palm trees,
White villas and white hotels
Fronting the beach and the sea
Seem most improbable to me

Whiling away the afternoon
In a cane rocking chair
On a small, secluded veranda,
Overrun with exotic flowers

I don't even know the names of,
Raised as I was by parents
Who kept the curtains drawn,
The lights low, the stove unlit,

Leaving me as wary as they'd be
At first seeing oranges in a tree,
Women running bare breasted
Over pink sands in a blue dusk.

MURKY MEMORIES

Mother is knitting me
A sweater in the dark.
Father is on all fours
Looking for a black cat.

HOUSE OF CARDS

I miss you winter evenings
With your dim lights.
The shut lips of my mother
And our held breaths
As we sat at a dining room table.

Her long, thin fingers
Stacking the cards,
Then waiting for them to fall.
The sound of boots in the street
Making us still for a moment.

There's no more to tell.
The door is locked,
And in one red-tinted window,
A single tree in the yard,
Leafless and misshapen.

IMPERSONATOR OF BLANK WALLS

Even as a child you sought to be invisible.
When it was time for dinner,
You went and hid under the bed
And let them search for you everywhere.

In school you liked erasers
More than you did pencils.
Empty rooms at dusk meant more to you
Than going to the movies.

Your date waited for you in the park,
While you sat in your kitchen
Cutting your head and neck
Out of old family photographs,

Giving yourself again the appearance
You had on snowy evenings,
Coming home to your parents
With your hair and eyebrows all white.

AUNT DINAH SAILED TO CHINA

Bearded ancestors, what became of you?
Have you gone and hid yourself
In some cabin in the woods
To listen to your whiskers grow in peace?

Clergymen patting chin curtains,
Soldiers with door knockers,
Sickly youths with goatees,
Town drunks proud of their ducktails.

Cousin Kate, was that a real moustache
You wore as you stood in church
Waiting for your bridegroom
To run up the stairs some day?

And you, grandpa, when you shouted at God
To do something about the world,
He kept quiet and let the night fall,
Seeing that your beard was whiter than his.

DOUBLES

In my youth, women often took me aside
And told me I reminded them of
A dead brother, an uncle, a late lover.
Some of them wore beards.
One lay with slashed wrists in a tub.
Another of my doubles had gone for a walk
And never came back from the woods.

It was evening; it was long ago, of course.
One played the piano beautifully
So that strangers knocked on his door.
Another went for a ride in a balloon.
The last time anyone saw me alive:
I was either wearing dark glasses
And reading the Bible on the subway,
Or crossing the street and laughing to myself.

TO LAZINESS

Only you understood
How little time we are given,
Not enough to lift a finger.
The voices on the stairs,
Thoughts too quick to pursue,
What do they all matter?
When eternity beckons.

The heavy curtains drawn,
The newspapers unread.
The keys collecting dust.
The flies either sluggish or dead.
The bed like a slow boat,
With its one listless sail
Made of cigarette smoke.

When I did move at last,
The stores were closed.
Was it already Sunday?
The weddings and funerals were over.
The one or two white clouds left
Above the dark rooftops,
Not sure which way to go.

THE GREAT DISAPPEARING ACT

One afternoon, you skipped school
To go for a swim in the river.
There were a few older boys there
Splashing around naked,
Their clothes in neat piles on the bank.

That time one of them hid yours as a joke.
You squatted in shallow water
Pleading, while they took their time
Combing their hair, getting dressed,
Then running off without a glance back.

Little by little it got dark and cold.
The lights went on in the city.
Still, you were going to wait a bit longer
Before stepping out of the river
To make a search among the rocks,

Or, if no luck, scale the embankment,
Dash naked over the railroad tracks,
Flit mothlike past the first lamppost,
Then let shadows lying in wait take you home
Along small streets lined with trees.

SUMMER DAWN

Just as the day breaks, it may be time
To slip away on foot
Carrying no belongings,
Leaving even your shoes behind
In some rooming house,
Or wherever you've hidden yourself away,

To look for another refuge,
Preferring at the moment
The open country, the interstate highway
Empty at this hour,
Or small-town cemeteries, where the birds
In the trees have fallen silent,

The minister has left the church unlocked.
You could enter and rest in its pews,
Or you could wade into a cornfield,
Swap clothes with a scarecrow,
Stretch out on the grass and have a long talk
With the first cloud of the new day.

II

GOURMETS OF TRAGEDIES

The season of fabulous feasts is coming.
Mouthwatering dishes of new evils
Are on the way to your table,
Its choicest morsels artfully broiled,

Steamed, deviled and stir-fried,
Elegantly arranged to seduce the eye
With fresh herbs and truffles
On plates flanked with wine glasses.

Have you made your choice?
The waiter will whisper as he lights the candles.
It will be June or January.
The one you adore will wear black.

The sight of spirits being poured
Over a saucepan and catching fire
Will make her close her eyes in bliss.
The righteous love to kill for their faith.

LISTEN

Everything about you,
My life, is both
Make-believe and real.
We are a couple
Working the night shift
In a bomb factory.

"Come quietly," one says
To the other
As he takes her by the hand
And leads her
To a rooftop
Overlooking the city.

At this hour, if one listens
Long and hard,
One can hear a fire engine
In the distance,
But not the cries for help,

Just the silence
Growing deeper
At the sight of a small child
Leaping out of a window
With its nightclothes on fire.

ENCYCLOPEDIA OF HORROR

Nobody reads it but the insomniacs.
How strange to find a child,
Slapped by his mother only this morning,
And the mad homeless woman
Who squatted to urinate in the street.

Perhaps they've missed something?
That smoke-shrouded city after a bombing raid,
The corpses like cigarette butts
In a dinner plate overflowing with ashes.
But no, everyone is here.

O were you to come, invisible tribunal,
There'd be too many images to thumb through,
Too many stories to listen to,
Like the one about guards playing cards
After they were done beating their prisoner.

SUNDAY

A birdbath on a darkening lawn.

Death playing tag
With someone's little boy,

Trampling on flower beds.

DANCE OF THE MACABRE MICE

"In the land of turkeys in turkey weather"
W. STEVENS

The president smiles to himself; he loves war
And another one is coming soon.
Each day we can feel the merriment mount
In government offices and TV studios
As our bombers fly off to distant countries.

The mortuaries are being scrubbed clean.
Soon they'll be full of grim young men laid out in rows.
Already the crowd gurgles with delight
At the bird-sweet deceits, the deep-throated lies
About our coming battles and victories.

Dark-clad sharpshooters on rooftops
Are scanning the mall for suspicious pigeons,
Blind men waving their canes in the air,
Girls with short skirts and ample bosoms
Reaching deep into their purses for a lighter.

FLYING HORSES

Neighbors leaned out of windows
To see a pretty girl pass by
While bombs fell out of the sky
And flames lit up the mirrors.

Our building was a roller coaster
We took a ride in every night
Wearing only our pajamas
And clutching a suitcase or a small dog.

It was like a street fair in hell.
Death had a shelf full of stuffed animals
At the shooting gallery
Where we were a row of ducklings

Marching in line with me tagging along,
Pulling a small toy truck by a string
While trying to make the sound of a motor
Rev up as it sits stuck in the mud.

IN THE HEAT OF THE NIGHT

Some long-haired youth, handcuffed,
Being led down the street
While the curious press close to see
And a cop lifts a club to whack him.

A gasp of surprise and satisfaction
That rose to your window
Till you sat up in bed, trembling,
Covered with sweat,
Fully awake, going over to look down
Into the boiling cauldron.

Fantastic species of shadow
Made their slow exodus
Over a high, fire-lit wall. The night air
Smelled of hot coals and grilled meat.

NIGHT WATCHMAN

"The Brain has Corridors"
E. D.

In a morgue of a city so large
I've never seen the end of it,
Or heard of anyone who did,
I make my rounds with a set of keys,
A flashlight and a black dog
Who's not allowed to be here,

But who knows not to bark
When the meat wagon comes,
And they wheel in their load,
Shutting doors to conceal
Their spooked, half-lit faces,
As they bend over the cadaver
On some business, leaving us

Once again in the dark, listening
To the soft hum of the refrigerators
As we prepare to resume our tour
Of padlocks, keyholes, empty offices
Where dusty files lie unopened
On small metal desks with squeaky chairs.

THE LIGHTS ARE ON EVERYWHERE

The Emperor must not be told night is coming.
His armies are chasing shadows,
Arresting whip-poor-wills and hermit thrushes
And setting towns and villages on fire.

In the capital, they go around confiscating
Clocks and watches, burning heretics
And painting the sunrise above the rooftops
So we can wish each other good morning.

The rooster brought in chains is crowing,
The flowers in the garden have been forced to stay open,
And still yet dark stains spread over the palace floors
Which no amount of scrubbing will wipe away.

MEMORIES OF THE FUTURE

There are one or two murderers in any crowd.
They do not suspect their destinies yet.
Wars are started to make it easy for them
To kill a woman pushing a baby carriage.

The animals in the zoo don't hide their worry.
They pace their cages or shy away from us
Listening to something we can't hear yet:
The coffin makers hard at work hammering the nails.

The strawberries are already in season
And so are the spring onions and radishes.
A young man buys roses, another rides
A bike through the traffic using no hands.

Old fellow bending over the curb to vomit,
Betake thee to thy own place of torment.
The sky at sunset is red with grilling coals.
A hand in a greasy potholder gropes after us over the rooftops.

COME WINTER

The mad and homeless take shelter
In stately tombs of the rich,
Where they cower in their rags,

And make themselves scarce
When a hearse happens along,
Bringing a whiff of freshly cut roses

And the sight of men in black
In a hurry to lower the heavy coffin
So it can ride Satan's luxury train

Where the swells kick off their shoes,
Wear funny hats and play lutes
As they gourmandize and sip wines,

While they roll through burning cities.
The huge crowds of the damned
Straining forward to catch a glimpse.

THOSE WHO CLEAN AFTER

for Robert Bly

Evil things are being done in our name.
Someone scrubs the blood,
As we look away,
Getting the cell ready for another day.

I can't make out their faces,
Only buckets and mops
Being carried down stone steps
Into the dark basement.

How quietly they hose the floor,
Unfurl the musty old rags
To wipe the hooks on the ceiling.
I hear only the sounds of summer night,

The leaves worried as always
By that nameless something
Which may be lurking out there
Where we used to keep the chickens.

IN THE JUNK STORE

A small, straw basket
Full of medals
From good old wars
No one recalls.

I flipped one over
To feel the pin
That once pierced
The hero's swelling chest.

MADMEN ARE RUNNING THE WORLD

Watch it spin like a wheel
And get stuck in the mud.

The truck is full of caged chickens
Squawking about their fate.

The driver has gone to get help
In a dive with a live band.

Myrtle, Phyllis, or whatever they call you girls!
Get some shut-eye while you can.

III

LATE-NIGHT CHAT

Of memory, the unhappy man's home.

How to guess time of night by listening to one's own heartbeat.

Why we can't see the end of our nose.

On the obscurity of words and clarity of things.

Why songbirds shit while they sing.

The truth about sneezing in church.

A few tips on how to make bad wine taste good.

What tunes to whistle while walking past a graveyard at night.

What to say to a mirror at four in the morning.

Plus a few thoughts regarding the little dolls she made that all looked like me.

How she stuck them with pins and hung them in a tree.

CLOUDS

To those worried about the future,
You bring tidings,
Shapes that may recall things
Without ever shedding
Their troubling ambiguity.

Like a troupe of illusionists
Traveling in circus wagons
You play hide-and-seek with the light
In country fairgrounds
Until overtaken by the night.

Taking a break from prophecy
Over small prairie towns
In company of dark trees,
Courthouse statues, crickets,
And other amateur ventriloquists.

IN THE AFTERNOON

The devil likes the chicken coop.
He lies on a bed of straw
Watching the snow fall.
The hens fetch him eggs to suck,
But he's not in the mood.

Cotton Mather is coming tonight,
Bringing a young witch.
Her robe already licked by flames,
Her bare feet turning pink
While she steps to the woodpile,

Saying a prayer; her hands
Like mating butterflies,
Or are they snowflakes?
As the smoke rises,
And the gray afternoon light returns

With its wild apple tree
And its blue pickup truck,
The one with a flat tire,
And the rusted kitchen stove
They meant to take to the dump.

ONE WING OF THE MUSEUM

Was empty. Even the guards were gone.
We strolled from room to room
Searching the blank walls in vain
Till we came to a row of windows
Overlooking an empty courtyard.
Rain had fallen; there was a puddle
Reflecting the wall and our window,

The two of us just barely visible,
Ghostlike looking from high up
At the wet cobblestones,
The one pigeon who appeared hurt,
Who wanted to be somewhere else
And did his best to get there,
Limping badly and stopping to rest.

PROPHESY

The last customer will stagger out of the door.
Cooks will hang their white hats.
Chairs will climb on the tables.
A broom will take a lazy stroll into a closet.

The waiters will kick off their shoes.
The cat will get a whole trout for dinner.
The cashier will stop counting receipts,
Scratch her ass with a pencil and sigh.

The boss will pour himself another brandy.
The mirrors will grow tired of potted palms
And darken slowly the way they always do
When someone runs off with a chicken.

DEAD RECKONING

He now found himself
In the company of a growing number
Of imponderables, which,
If they ever allow themselves
To be understood, do so
Only with great reluctance.

The more he reflected on things,
The more he felt sure
Of nothing, except
His being here,
Holding on for dear life
To a few eccentricities.

Like his inability to sleep at night.
A lifelong rebellion
Against that monster Eternity.
A desire now and then
To raise his head from the pillow
And spit in its eye in the dark.

METAPHYSICS ANONYMOUS

A storefront mission in a slum
Where we come together at night
To confess our lifelong addiction
To truth beyond appearances,
Of which there are clues everywhere,

Or so we tell ourselves.
Estranged from family and friends,
Busy tuning pianos on Saturn,
Looking for a moonbeam in a cucumber,
If you were to ask us.

The unreality of us being here,
An additional quandary we are cautioned
Not to bother our heads with
As we wait with eyes lowered
For coffee and cookies to be served.

HIGH WINDOWS

Sky's gravedigger.
Bird catcher,
Dark nights' match seller—
Or whatever you are?

A book-lined tomb,
Pots and pans music hall.
Insomnia's sick nurse,
Burglar's blind date,

And you
Stripper's darkened stage
Next to a holy martyr
Being flayed by the setting sun.

GHOST SHIP

The soul is a ghost ship
Set adrift on the seas of eternity,
Its one remaining mast
A cross on a pauper's grave
You hold on to like a drunk,
Counting the little white caps
As they chase one another
Like butterflies downwind.

With no land in sight,
Evenings, dressed for dinner,
You lean over a pool table
As the ship pitches and rolls,
The glasses tinkle in the bar
And the potted palms sway
While a jazz band plays the blues
On a badly scratched record.

At midnight, you'll rise and walk
The length of the old wreck,
Peeking into each dark porthole,
Searching for your cabin
And catching sight of your face,
Pale like the moon, then blurring
With each high, crashing wave.

WONDERS OF THE INVISIBLE WORLD

Wine had bloodied your lips and tongue,
When you whispered your tale
Of how young witches
Used to ride married men
Through the sky on a night like this.

The stars were like lit candles
That had wandered off on their own,
And the misty woods
Were full of floating nightgowns.
It seemed only yesterday
Old Scratch tucked us into a bed of dead leaves.

You turned into a black cat
And I ran after you on all fours
Into a church where a dog chased us
And the congregation sat
With their grave faces looking on.

SECRET HISTORY

Of the light in my room:
Its mood swings,
Dark-morning glooms,
Summer ecstasies.

Spider on the wall,
Lamp burning late,
Shoes left by the bed,
I'm your humble scribe.

Dust balls, simple souls
Conferring in the corner.
The pearl earring she lost,
Still to be found.

Silence of falling snow,
Night vanishing without trace,
Only to return.
I'm your humble scribe.

WIRE HANGERS

All they need
Is one little red dress
To start swaying
In that empty closet

For the rest of them
To nudge each other,
Clicking like knitting needles
Or disapproving tongues.

TO THE READER

Don't you hear me
Bang my head
Against your wall?

Of course, you do,
So how come
You don't answer me?

Bang your head
On your side of the wall
And keep me company.

THE ICE CUBES ARE ON FIRE

In a kitchen with blinds drawn,
The woman bent over a sink,
Rubbing ice cubes over her face,
Stops to peek through a slit.

A neighbor's dog is loose
Sniffing around the trash cans,
Happy to be free of his chain
On this day of sweltering heat,

Or so she thinks as she resumes
Cooling her throat and shoulders,
Shivering down to her painted toes,
Her eyes shut against the sun.

LABOR AND CAPITAL

The softness of this motel bed
On which we made love
Demonstrates to me in an impressive manner
The superiority of capitalism.

At the mattress factory, I imagine,
The employees are happy today.
It's Sunday and they are working
Extra hours, like us, for no pay.

Still, the way you open your legs
And reach for me with your hand
Makes me think of the Revolution,
Red banners, crowd charging.

Someone stepping on a soapbox
As the flames engulf the palace,
And the old prince in full view
Steps to his death from a balcony.

THE BLUR

He lost the thread of his story in a forest,
So he went down on his knees to search for it

When he saw a blur of light between the trees,
Like a wedding gown made of cobwebs,

The unknown bride setting out for a stroll
In a graveyard where her people lie buried—

Or so he let himself be fooled once—
And now couldn't think of anything else to say.

THE BATHER

Where the path to the lake twists
Out of sight, a puff of dust,
The kind bare feet make running.
A low branch heavy with leaves
Swaying momentarily
In the dense and somber shade.

A late bather disrobing for a dip,
Pinned hair coming undone soon to float
As she flips on her back letting
The sleepy current take her
Over the dark water to where the sky
Opens wide, the night blurring

Her nakedness, the silence thick,
Treetops like charred paper edges,
Even the insects oddly reclusive,
The rare breath of wind in the leaves
Fooling me to look once again,
Until the chill made me rise and go in.

CRICKETS

Blessed are those for whom
Time doesn't run
Into dark of night,
But drags its feet,

A moment's captive,
Like a lone sail
At sunset
Suspended on the bay,

A few gulls in the sky
Keeping it company,
And closer to home,
Crickets, crickets, crickets.

IV

ETERNITIES

Discreet reader of discreet lives.
Chairs no one ever sits in.
Motes of dust, their dancing days done.
Schools of yellow fish
On the peeling wallpaper
Keeping their eyes on you.
It's late for today, late.
A small crucifix over the bed
Watches over a stopped clock.

★

Sewing room, linty daylight
Through a small window.
You will never be in my shoes, Eternity.
I come with an expiration date.
My scissors cut black cloth.
I stick silver pins into a tailor's dummy,
Muttering some man's name
While aiming at its heart.

★

Raleigh played cards with his executioners.
I sit over a dead mouse in the kitchen.
Hot night, the windows open,
The air rich with the scents of lilacs
And banked fires of backyard grills.
My lovely neighbor must be sleeping naked,
Or lighting a match to see what time it is.

★

The torment of branches in the wind.
Is the sea hearing their confession?
The little white clouds must think so.
They are rushing over to hear.
The ship on the way to paradise
Seems stuck on the horizon,
Pinned by one golden pin of sunlight.
Only the great rocks act as if nothing's the matter.

★

In a city where so much is hidden:
The crimes, the riches, the beautiful women,
You and I were lost for hours.
We went in to ask a butcher for directions.
He sat playing the accordion.
The lambs had their eyes closed in bliss,
But not the knives, his evil little helpers.
Come right in, folks, he said.

★

Conscience, that awful power,
With its vast network of spies,
Secret arrests at night,
Dreaded prisons and reform schools,
Beatings and forced confessions,
Wee-hour crucifixions.
A small, dead bird in my hand
Is all the evidence they had.

★

The sprawling meadow bordered by a stream,
Naked girl on horseback.
Yes, I do remember that.
Sunlight on the outhouse wall,
One little tree in the yard afraid of darkness,
The voice of the hermit thrush.

★

Thoughts frightened of the light,
Frightened of each other.
They listen to a clock ticking.
Like flock of sheep led to slaughter,
The seconds keep a good pace,
Stick together, don't look back,
All worried, as they go,
What their shepherd may be thinking.

★

A sough of wind in the open window
Making the leaves sigh.
"I come to you like one
Who is dying of love,"
God said to Christine Ebner
On this dull, sultry night.
"I come to you with the desire
Of bridegroom for his bride."

★

Soul's jukebox
Playing golden oldies
In the sky
Strewn with stars.
When I ask God
What size coin it takes
I'm greeted
With stunned silence.

ETERNITY'S ORPHANS

One night you and I were walking.
The moon was so bright
We could see the path under the trees.
Then the clouds came and hid it
So we had to grope our way
Till we felt the sand under our bare feet,
And heard the pounding waves.

Do you remember telling me,
"Everything outside this moment is a lie"?
We were undressing in the dark
Right at the water's edge
When I slipped the watch off my wrist
And without being seen or saying
Anything in reply, I threw it into the sea.

Some of these poems have previously appeared in the following magazines to whose editors grateful acknowledgment is made: *London Review of Books*, *The New Yorker*, *The American Scholar*, *Poetry Ireland*, *Verse*, *Boulevard*, *Virginia Quarterly Review*, *Five Points*, *Poetry*, *The New York Review of Books*, *TLS*, *Jubilat*, *Daedalus*, *Tri-Quarterly*, *Notre Dame Review*, *The New Ohio Review*, and *Southwest Review*.